ENDLESS THRESHOLD

by Jack Hirschman

CURBSTONE PRESS

8 8 6 7 0

26153468

FIRST EDITION, 1992
Copyright © 1992 by Jack Hirschman
ALL RIGHTS RESERVED

PS 3558
.I 68 E5
1992

Cover photograph by Rob Lee
Cover design by Stone Graphics
Printed in the U.S. by Princeton University Press

Some of these poems have appeared in: *The American Poetry Review, Ampersand, Bachy, Bullhorn, Compages, Enclitic, The Equator, Howl, Inky Blue, Left Curve, Literary Review, Long Shot, The Minneapolis Review of Baseball, Nexus, Onthebus, The Pacific Coast News, The People's Tribune, Poet News, Poetry USA* and *The Tenderloin Times*.

Curbstone Press is a 501(c)(3) nonprofit literary arts organization whose operations are supported in part by private donations and by grants from the ADCO Foundation, the Connecticut Commission on the Arts, the Andrew W. Mellon Foundation, the National Endowment for the Arts, and the Plumsock Fund.

ISBN: 1-880684-00-4
Library of Congress number: 91-58996

distributed by
InBook
Box 120261
East Haven, CT 06512

published by
CURBSTONE PRESS
321 Jackson Street
Willimantic, CT 06226

for our gentle comrades

Contents

ENDLESS THRESHOLD

Endless Threshold

The fears:
that the poem will be
entangled
in the web
of protocol,
that the word will lose
meaning as
soulfact
in the struggle
to reveal by
propaganda,
that we are here
as presences
without wings
or altitude,
that creation
is a job
like any other,
that the future,
because
it's without
foundation in
anything
but the real,
is the end
of feeling

as we were
taught to feel,
that we are
the turning
upon the axle
of new self-dint,
sparks
in the womb
of collective being,
that the real
is not illusion,
that there is
the groundswell
of a process
such as never
felt before,
that we cannot
return, as if
to a past love,
to the left breast
of a sect
or the right-on
of a pun,
that we are
adrift
catching only
the drift
of the thing
up ahead,
knowing it exists
yet hard put

to uncover it all,
hold all of it
in our hands
for fear
it will kill us,
yet always aware
it is irresistible
because at last
we are able
to see with eyes
infused with
the greater purport
that its clarity
has dazzled away
the dross in us
and set us free
to be
psychopomps
and guardians
of its inmost demands.

O in this
neverbefore
quite-like,
in this
seemingly
inch-by-inch
where we target,
strike and chip
at the hard rock
where we've heard

the stirring
of an alchemy
surpassing gold
or uranium,
we are like
motherless
bastards deep
in the earth,
orphan miners
such as
neverbefore
worked the depths
of the need
to transform,
born from
everyone tortured,
martyred and
starving,
caged in labors
of slaves
or in the common
cage of despair,
homeless
with nothing
but street,
hungry
with nothing
but palm —

Look,
everywhere

and wherever
in this dark
pit we must out,
not simply
look out
for our own
self-interested
intellectual skins,
we must out
of our skins
with the hammer
of the agitating
work, break
through schist,
plough up veins,
clear paths
to the trapped
but stirring
moil of a mass
of heartbreaks
already
in motion
everywhere and
wherever —
there is a
thunder in us
greeting
the thunder
underlying
the motion
of those

with nothing
but a sense
of the chain-
breaking storm.
Let's go
deeper!
The rest is
death's life
and death's
fences,
the tick of
the buck
like a deathknell
on every instant.
The rest is
thunderless dread,
the poem
on its knees,
gutless acrylic,
ideas dying
to be furniture
plush with
the fat of the ass,
music that means
nothing and unfurls
nothing's flag
and salutes
nothing's star
and is in fact
nothing's rags.

We have been
that,
now all
and fearlessly
forward
deepening
and widening
let's go!

We already
have made
our road
endless
threshold.

All hands
to the
crossing!

That Poet

That poet you admire so —

in my fifteen years
in the workers' movement
I've never seen him
in attendance at
a demonstration against
social injustice, or at
a memorial honoring
a revolutionary hero,
or at a rally in support
of an uprising people —

is not even a *fighting*
surrealist
but a bibelot
dribbling over
with obsolete pus.

The Halls of Academe

You see, there is the structure
of the lonely confirmation of learned indignity.
The dodecaphony of retreat plays through
its walls.
Its printing presses publish the masters
from one end of the spectrum to another,
books written in oil now
for the intelligence,
for the intelligence
must not be stupid.
Stupid is the hooker-mad street
where one sloshes around
in blood money.
Stupid is the reified concrete
where one presumes to say something.
There is nothing to say.
No ism is cooler than the water
in a footpedal fountain in one of its halls.
Meaning is nothing but the urge
to remain away from
the land of one's birth.
Even its airports are filled with art,
even its banks,
and there the motion and the money
seem washed as a brain
in one of its countless lecture rooms,

washed spanking white
as the bare ass of a platonic thought.
You see, once there,
there's no turning back because
everything is a turned back,
an intellectual stab,
a sodomy of mind.

And nobody here, in part,
is not there,
since the two giant corporations
began groping each other,
and television wrote off the eyes,
and record albums brought back illiteracy,
and even the hookers were turned out
to song and dance
on the covers of pornography.

Stupid, from the top of, the head of
the cock of, the state down
to the two sacs
of the ball-carrying

flat-feet come:
megabux or
measly man,
exiled forever
from home.

The Painting

So there it is:
a painting of the late Black heroic
mayor of Chicago
in woman's underwear
in the name of artistic iconoclasm
and free expression
and constitutional liberty
and individual civil rights.

And there they are at last,
the city aldermen
taking it off the walls
removing it from the exhibition
in the name of the working masses
whose constitutional liberties
and free expression
and civil rights

have been smothered, censored,
bribed, shunted, overlooked;
and now whose heroes
are made into kitsch,
pornogrified, transvesticized
to reflect the most cheapshot
degrading and racially humiliating
business-as-usual nation on earth.

Well, what do you say?
Were they wrong to remove the painting
of the progressive mayor
who'd led the working people
toward destruction
of a rotting fascist machine
that wants to re-assert
its disgusting oppression
now that Harold Washington is dead?
Bubububut removing a painting!
Bubububut the artist's individual . . .
the artist's individu
the artist's individ
the artist's indiv
the artist's in
Whawhawhawhat about the artist?

What about the class?

Provoprovoprovoprovocation is the essence of art!

Provocation for what, Mr. Curator?
Mr. Institutional Curator.
Mr. Corporate-Funded Institutional Curator.
Mr. Elite Corporate-Funded Institutional Curator.
Provocation for what?

Bubububut what about the empty wallspace, the violation
of the artist, the damage to culture. . . !

You are the empty wallspace, Mr. Curator,
you are the violation of the artist
and the damage to culture.
David Nelson painted *Mirth & Girth*
out of the hundred twisted fantasies
of the sleaze of politics and the politics of sleaze,
of the terror of the sex of Blackness
and the Blackness of sex —
fantasies used by capitalism
secretly through racist aesthetics
or openly through the markets of porn
to displace imagination with a price,
to keep artists and workers alike
filthy in their purity,
paralyzed in dirty-minded liberty,
fugitives from human dignity
and political struggle,
stupefied when confronting collective life
or revolutionary action.

We are partisan, Mr. Make-It Curator,
and you, Mr. Make-It-New Artist,
we're at war
with art as privilege,
with the kitsching up of the soul,
with the gooning of the truth
about those who help working people see
how beautiful the reality
of their imagination as a class
in motion actually is.

Do we acclaim the removal of the painting?
Emphatically, provocatively
Yes!

Paiute Ant Pudding

They would go in deep night before the ants were awake
with an empty sack and another with burning coals.
They would stuff the branches where the ants were sleeping,
into the empty sack, scrape them down,
and pour them into the sack with the burning coals.
The legs and pincers would come loose in the heat.
Back in camp, they would empty the tiny bodies
on a mat of leather, wash them clean with water,
and with flour and hot water make a gravy
which would cool into a pudding by daybreak.
A hundred years later, this ant pudding can still
rise off the ground or a modern table
and fling itself at the face of any fucking Nazi.

Up South

for Anna Kithcart

Up south, I can tell you,
I remember what was done
to the finest artist in the land,
I'm talking about Paul Robeson
                          up south
in the state of New York

Up south, I can tell you,
I remember what we did
to that poor Black woman
when I was a kid
in a gang in a cellar
                          up south
in New York City
in the state of New York

My heritage is Black
from that night forward;
my Jewish: Black,
my Hebrew: Black,
my Joyce and Hemingway
and Thomas: Black
from that night forward
                          up south
in New York City
in the state of New York

Anna Kithcart — she knows
but will never say,
so let me say it for her:
DEATH TO THE KLAN!
Tawana Brawley — she knows
and her silence shouts out:
DEATH TO THE KLAN!
On the day the Howard Beach
thugs were acquitted,
with my Black brothers I cry:
DEATH TO THE KLAN!
and the system that protects it
in police stations,
in assemblies of government,
in the governor's mansion
                                    up south
in the state of New York

Death to the weapon of terror
that divides worker from worker
and worker from work!
Death to its secret practitioners
and their means of production
and their rotten lipservice
in the state of New York
and in California too

The lonesomest beauty in this land
was brutally murdered last week
by those who want to keep your poems
bric-a-brac in your cheeks,

by those who want to burn a cross
in a field of change just sown
and incinerate the seeds
budding 'round Jesse Jackson

She was our sister, our daughter,
our girl and our blood —
How long? and how many?
No more from now.
I put this in the form of a vow:
The buds shall blossom,
that cross shall die
beneath our united dowse,
and the land harvest its crop
of revolutionary springtimes
up and down south.

Black Belt

I hear the righteous truth
of Albert Turner emerge
from the cinders of his burned house
and the ballot Exes rise
from the humiliated land acquitted of fraud.

Vote heart vote simple blues
Vote downhome trees with leaves
full of trees in miniature
and such trees wet with tears
for the strange fruit and the years and the years.

The Tremor

Two young guys
in the rear of a San Francisco bus
loudly interweaving
raucous talk about
  food food food,
  tacos smeared with hotsauce,
  pizza to make them
  "full as fuck,"

their obscenities frightening
the eyes of the children
sitting nearby, sensitive as books,
on either side of their mother.

Allover town handshakes
are turning into panhandles.

"Food, food, muthuhfuckin'
food's what it's all about!"

The dying, the lies
written in the eyes
and at the corners
of the mouths allaround.

Just below the pursed lips,
the twist,
        the truth
cursed by control, terrorized
into taut silence.

"Food, food, muthufuckin'
food's what it's all about!"
— brash, noisy, dashing
everything
        (books, newspapers, thoughts)
against the bus windows.
because they're hungry
and they want their lust for food
to get down and in under everybody's skin,
they want the whole bus to know
they're hungry
and their hunger
is forever being beaten down,
pommelled and spat upon
every day of their lives.

Sometimes
I can be so still,
I can feel
the trembling of my age, the earthquake
of the young demanding the justice
a decrepit generation
of hustlers and thieves
were forced to rob them of,

as their generation
and the generation before theirs had been robbed,
and I unite with the coming tremor.

Earthworks

1.

It is a style of work
our science breeds,
a priceless clarity.

"Turn from the roots of death,"
cries the Muse of the Fearful.

Matter, we're not afraid,
we are of Thee a part.
The thought that matters
is itself matter.
So also the heart.

And these syllables.
And the next.

Earthquake.

In the aftershocks that nourish
quiet panics, pains, painkillers,
thanksgivings in the dark,
glasses clink: To Life!

"After death, a formal feeling comes . . ."
We're never without it, it is

the unspoken reason why we gather
to speak together, to unite with
the what-must-be-done,
to struggle to disclose
the collapses, obstructions
and rubbish that keeps us
wedged between
doubt and superstition,
to lift them into the open
so that they cease
once and for all
their backward shibboleth.

Dialectical materialism means, among other things,
the dispossession
of death.

2.

Standing at the corner
of Columbus & Green Streets
with Kristen Wetterhahn
a week after the quake,

I saw the people walking
still dazed from within

in a slow stunned drift
of apprehension,

and I remarked they seemed
as in Bucharest,
which we'd visited
in 1980,

35 years after the War
and the burden
of their near-destruction
still upon them

a week after the quake
in San Francisco.
The War was like the quake
and our fear

that it will come again
suddenly showed me 40 years
of slow streets and a pungent
tangibility behind the curtain

we called Iron. Ironically now
since the chips and discs
are falling where they may
in a world less fragile than a star.

3.

Like dissonance inward
these days
                of cicatrices widening,
cracks in bridges, unsteady stones,
a wobble within
as if soul had been
                aftershook,
an almost tangible dread:
the taste of totality on our lips.

Dry sweat.
Anxious sunshine.
The interval between
two thunders.

There is a masterwork by Webern.
37 seconds it lasts.

Chance suddenly jumped,
upagainst
the motherfucking wall
of premeditation.

A fire engine still screams
toward 15 seconds
two weeks ago.

Clangs toll.
Sirens riptooth through the night
and shorten every breath.

Crude slang at the corners
of the mouth conceals
a gasping for air,
an under-rubbled moan.

That whiff of.
Autumnal essence.
Heart-stilts
fundamental now.

Sunsong

Sun, good.
Bright sun.
Warm and healthy
sun.
Come again tomorrow
because I'm dark
all day.
Play on my body
on the grass;
and on my belly
in my bed
near the window
of the room
in the old hotel until nightfall.
Stay.

October 11, 1990

It was a happy day
when he was born
34 years ago
my blond son.

How golden the sun
in the park today,
how happy the birds
and flying balls.

I sit in golden light
almost forgetting
he's eight years gone
because the sun

is so like his hair
and the air like
the golden laughter
of his love.

Eight years old and
into a radiant windup.
Here comes a perfect
strike of light

upon an old old glove.

The Jacket

(in memory of Leopoldo Fiorenzato,
suicided 1987)

All day
I have been moiled
with the most insipid self-drowning
blindness of
sentimentality.

Then I looked up
from the bed
where I work on my back.
On the closet door
directly in front of me
I had hung my jacket.
Half of the sleeve
had gotten squashed
into the armhole
and its wrinkling formed
a wink at that point,
while the rest of the sleeve
hung down like a nose
ending in a nostril
just above the inscrutable
slit-smile of the pocket.
The whole face hung
from the corner of the door
like a magnificent

dummy, the head almost
coming to a point.
The point is,
it saved me from
that prick Jack Hirschman
lying there full
of 65,000 lies about
himself and the world
per drop of sperm.
Ciao, Leopoldo.

Dream

I stood on the ash-heap over
the lot across the street —
10 years old —
with broomstick bat in one hand,
a chunk of ash in the other,
in lone fungo sadness
near twilite.

I wake, but the legs of my friend
Neil are still burning
from the windy tarpaper matchstick
accident,

the long flaming scarf around him
in the gutter,
his little bulldog barking,

his screams and hands trying
to tear it from his body
and me standing there, terrified,
doing nothing.

43 years later I get out of bed.

I still don't know why.

Asa

I can't conceive of you that way
without my skull filling with our belly laughter,
                          and the curve
of a dirtpath down the lots at the end of a street
                          in The Bronx.

Old friend, see what you went and did?
kicked the bucket with your tin leg
down the long final stoop, and the dead neighborhood
came alive as if for a fire

Now I carry a head at my side, thigh-high,
in my hands held up to the sun,
on my shoulder, on my arm,
in my thought at the tip of my pen
I carry an essence of Asa
who was brother though not blood,
a palm on the shoulder of childhood,
a sway of the magic of the poem,
who went off to war
and living afterward in exile
kept a fingerpoint on me
that made the island far away next door.

For a spell of years we travelled the poem together,
though continents apart, by in and exhaling

gematrias of the art of the jazz of words —
                "Chances are . . ."
                        Chance *hasard*
                        Chance is czar

about covers it,
and the design therein
of all those paths where seraphs and serifs
and *sephers* multiplied.

I'll always see him, arms widespread, skipping and jumping
at the top of the steps of the sublime stoop,
which were the forms of his poems themselves,
put together, mundane with arcane,
by his lifting of the letters by the seats of their pants,
turning them over and inside out,
making pacts with the absences within and between them,
dancing them down to the pitchpenny street
and through the cracks making books
of pinpointedly succinct sophisticated alchemies
that could mint new Abrahams at the bottom
                        of the Yellow River
in the Third Century B.C., and make them sound
like daffodils on Hebden Heath.

It was always bright darkness when Asa at table
spelled out the lineage of alphabets and trees,

dazzling the babblers with his style of understatement,
perfectly inserted like a synchrony,

and the seams of paranoia would split at his hip
deep self-deprecations,

and the wood as if hypnotized stripped to its
mystic glyphs

Now he's supposed to be one with the spaces
                              between and around
and within the letters he most adored,
a style and content at last,
but the bucket's anxious racket as it tumbles
sounds like Fire!
and the ladders called out simply won't lie down
precisely because they're also your poems

I just can't conceive of you that way
without my skull filling with our belly laughter,
                              and the curve
of a dirtpath down the lots at the end of a street
                              in The Bronx.

A little kid can turn on it
with a stompy clomp of dust,
in knee-pants, tee-shirt,
knickers in the fall.

You did.
Me too.

Meet you there after school.

Nellie

After his shouts, the strops, her screams, the thrown things,
the doorslam, the bitter weeping,
out of the thin box, as the delicate paper was parted,
she'd lift the sheer mojud stockings
and run her fingertips along them,
slowly smiling girlishly again.

She'd begin singing a Perry Como song,
she loved Perry Como and would sing
the same song he sang, all day long,
on the Make-Believe Ballroom Time.

Then, in a black brassiere strapped to her freckled shoulders,
she'd sit on the bed, fit the stockings,
stand up and notch them to the garters
that hung down from her black girdle.
A ripple of fat ran round her waist, squeezed out
by the girdle, different from
the plumps that swelled out from her brassiere.
And I saw a blue bruise, the shadow
of a belt-buckle on her thigh.

But she was singing again, and over the girdle
she'd put on a pair of pink bloomers,
and over everything, then, a brown-and-white flower-print
summer-golden dress.

Her white heels had holes in the toes where her nail-polish
showed through. The bottle of polish, tweezers, lipstick,
rouge, brush and emeryboard were on the vanity table
over there looking in the mirror.

Her lips swam in the Como song with rose-red strokes,
reaching the end with a shiny glow,
like the waxy cameo of her mother
on the brooch in the drawer.

She'd hold out her hand and say, "Come, darling . . ."

We'd walk hand in hand up and down our street
                    in the twilight,
and the neighbors would cry out: "Hi, Nellie!" or "Hello,
Mrs. Hirschman," and "Hi, Jackie. My, how you've grown!"

The Prince

for my father, Steve Hirschman

I slipped the birthday card (there was a space
between the stone wall at the bleachers' end
and the bullpen fencing just above it in left field
in the old Yankee Stadium)
to George Caster, relief pitcher sitting on
a bench just below even
11 year-old me,
asking would he give it to Hal Newhouser
when the game was over, would he, please?
It was May 29, 1945.
My Tigers were in first and going to win the World
Series.

When I heard that you, my favorite southpaw, poppa,
no longer can walk, the pain
is too much,
46 years later, it all comes back to me, down to
the pock-marked smile on Caster's face
as he took the envelope,
and the high kick and wing of lefty Prince Hal
in the distance firing
a wicked fast ball from the mound,
and the big sound of your cry
"Strike Three!"
over my shoulder.

A Recognition

Sitting at a table in Specs
I glanced at the bar
and saw a young guy made me say:
Sandy Auslander!
No, the son of Sandy Auslander!
because Sandy Auslander
was a kid I knew
in The Bronx;
and then it came to me: why
did I think of Sandy Auslander
after all these years, Sandy
Auslander whom I wasn't
particularly close to or fond of,
with his swarthy somewhat
bullishly overstuffed bearing,
a left-fielder but actually
better on the football field —
but that wasn't the point,
the point was: why
did I think this young guy
was — even for a moment —
the son of Sandy Auslander?
Was it simply that I was
looking for David
and had quite naturally
transferred generation

to the Auslanders, to feel
what it would be like
to feel again the recognition
of the father in the living
son in the emptiness
of knowing my son was dead?
That still would not explain
why the name Sandy Auslander
came to me in a flash
after forty years, years
when I was young
and had not even married
or fathered a child.
Why Sandy Auslander?
Why not another, closer
friend of childhood
and adolescence?
Why had that young guy
(who by this time had left
the cafe) called to mind
the name of someone
I had not thought about
for these same forty years?
Some latency at puberty
reinvoked perhaps?
Perhaps it was the dark
almost latino skin
that made me realize
that everyone in that gang
of kids was fair or light-skinned
(except, of course, Maurice Kohl

who was always dirty
and whom we called Bituminous)
but for Sandy Auslander
who was darker even
than the Italians,
more like a Puerto Rican
coming into the neighborhood
or what today you'd call
a Palestinian. Perhaps that
was why. Yet all the perhapses
left the matter unresolved.
I left the cafe after a while,
went to my hotel, got into bed
and began writing the poem
you are reading or listening to.
Three thousand miles from
my childhood in New York,
forty years from the time
I was lead to the book.
Life is a desert of miracles.
I just heard the corny rhyme
of my sweet sad father.
Darling, I long to see you,
my mother cries.

The Foundation

There was a boy my age named Tommy Ricchio
lived a block away in The Bronx. I don't know,
I must have been five or six, seven at most,
it was summer I was in short pants and can still
feel the cool and the swelter on my legs,
and from Tommy Ricchio, like it was straight
out of his heart to me, there came this very pure light.
It happened on the hill in front of his tenement
where a bunch of us boys were standing around playing —
maybe I'd said or done something, I don't remember,
I can't even remember what Tommy Ricchio looked like
since he didn't play with us much and I saw him only
a few times more, around the schoolyard, as we grew up,
from a distance; but the very pure light —
I felt it go inside me, I felt him go inside me, —
it was the first time, more radiant than the sun,
I knew I had a brother.

Cheryl Araujo

When she died
in an orgasm
of fender, tree, sunburst
and bourbon scream

Cheryl Araujo's spirit
flew from the hands
of the players
a cuestick of fire
burning into the green
of the table, crying:

Cheryl Araujo is dead
she always was cold
she had it coming
and you gave it to her
on the green table
like six bullets
in a gun
but she was a bitch
for life
she wouldn't die
and now she barks
from the other side
that your drink
and your dope

your crosses and speed
your gang rapes
and paranoia
finally took the wheel
drove her drove her
totalled Cheryl Araujo
dead.

Two kids leftover
run around
with their heads
chopped off.

Six cocks crow
in cages
but nothing dawns.

America, you night
of bats and rocks

and garbage under
your white sheets.

The wooden sticks
between your legs.

Your blind blue chalk.

Loving

She is a languid mouth
making up
before my cock
with a hundred lipsticks,
is a tongue-tied wide-open throat
with no end of hunger,
is the faster who slowly devours
surrender without religion,
is the lush of cum
with a twist of whisper,
is the frothy horse
who rides my dark crop,
is the belch of laughter,
sublime labor's yawn,
the fart of hope
in this field rotted by mind
and the tics of palaver,
she is my blind sight
without a stitch of death on
though I bury my spasms in her
with all my sad grave things.

Zexpome

O plum, you round
of juices that sing in me,

who am the pits,
come, break your plunge on me,

I want my dregs opened,
my ferment spiced by your lips,

my fondlebone giving you
swim for swum,

O plum, you round
double-blush in my palms.

Innerunder

"Not the declaration which is the truth
but the thing which is." — George Oppen

It comes down to this:
there's no
principle to the thing;
it's what it is
and thus can be
used to be
gotten used to,

which begets
gottenyu,

which is where
world is now.

Nowhere
I can look outside
the borders of the lie
now.

Lie with me, love,
that's the only where
for a while we're
no thing
and grow slowly true
the way becoming

to each other is
supposed to:

a flesh beside, or upon,
and all the imagings

innerunder can do
wonders in the places
where we're dead,
kneading our bodies
like bread,
the days' rags
and shards

cobbled together
into these moments
you touch my hobble-stick
and I your hovelled
heart with a kiss
still-warm.

Not for nothing
most of body is water
even as teevee grows
in every brain.

So it went
and I went with it
and here I am
again with it, spent

like a broken old
buffalo & Indian
nickel, outwardly
undented.

The Weeping

Walking to my room from the park
where I'd been sunning
my words on a bench with a buddy,
I passed a couple of women
and it seemed to me
as they walked and talked
they were weeping.

I continued on, and another
woman passed, and she too
seemed to have come
from somewhere mournful,
her eyes at once dry and yet
inconspicuously weeping.

I looked this way and that
at the corner, hoping
to find the source
of the sudden feeling
that someone had died,
someone I knew in the neighborhood,
but I could find nothing.

Could it have been your despair,
dear woman with whom I've lived
but live no longer,

two hours before you came to visit
and tell of it? Could your wandering
mournfulness have come to me
in the glisten of those women's eyes?

O friend, see, even as we
stroke our bliss
of sadness away,
a blush subsists
under the sallow
skins of one or another
of our addictions,
like the unforgettable blush
on that woman's face
in the hotel corridor
in the small town
in Romania
in the morning,
lactic with roses,
innocent and enduring and smiling
as if she had something
profoundly to do
with the awful physical night
of smoke and poisons and violence
that we are forced every day
to lug along with our bodies
into the sunlight.

Chinatown

Two Chinese women
squatting on the sidewalk
having a confab.

Manioc stems
like wooden
puppets,

blue-clawed
crabs
in paper bags,

persimmon
suns in
a stall.

Human Interlude

for Terry Garvin

She was standing against
      the wall near
the Tevere Hotel holding
      a plastic cup
as it began to rain.

I dug for a coin, walked
      up to her
and dropped it in.
      It fell to the bottom
of an orange drink.

I blushed, looked into her
      ravaged eyes and skin
          and hair prematurely
greying, and said
I was sorry, I'd thought

she needed some bread.
      "I do," she said
and smiled, "I was
      just having a little
         drink."

And we stood there
      laughing together

as we watched the raindrops fall
on the orange lake
above the drowning money.

The Two Women

As I was eating
inside, the door of
the cafe opened
and the Chinese woman
in the rain stood
under a large black
umbrella. The woman
dishwasher greeted her
inside, the umbrella
closed but their chatter
opened to include
the men at the counter
with jibes and wristpats,
peppering the wet
and hungry evening
with laughter
and a woolworth-bijou
admiration close
as a neighborhood
before the eyes
beholding.

Civic Center

On the ledge that runs along the flank
of the San Francisco Public Library,
two of them lay in the sunlight:
two long and tall cardboard boxes
like caskets for two homeless people
who had gone into the toothless sunlight
scavenging and begging along the Loin
among the other stubble no razor
can keep from growing, and cuts
and blood and punctures and suck-wrist
terrors and the hickies on the neck
above a simple cross of wood between
breasts in a doorway of a dead grocery.

Skid Row Scene

At the skid row corner
where the corner
of the mouth
            is blood
            or bloodied
and the wall next
to the liquor store
knows the ragged
or frayed backs
and twos or threes
or bunches even
of young and old
stand around
hip or flip talkin',
women there too
in lively waste,
a crutch leaning
against a window,
someone about to
give up, that is, flop down —
anyway, in the midst
comes this bespectacled
Black man in porkpie hat,
blue serge suit, beige
raincoat, walking slowly
with a hook-shaped aluminum

cane in his hand.
At the scraggy, winey
corner, he is like
a very fine point of jazz
as if forever impeccably strolling
thru the downtown anywhere of funk junk
and lunks, with a little broken swank
and a sense of historical flair.

In Memoriam
Ray Thompson (1943-1990)

Of the streets,
of begging hands and windblown cardboard,
of flophouse doorways or the lot behind the autobody shop,
of evictions from one downpour to another
and the trembling coffee,
the burning corner can,
the scavenged alleys,
the scratched and ravaged graffiti,
the transient handbills
and collectives of alone,

he was a poet
who wrote the deep lines the rotting weather
of this system cuts into human faces,
who saw in the cracks and the fissures
endurance birthing flashes of a radiant
lava-whirl of erupting rage,
and how hungry hunger is for it!
how widespread homelessness is for it!
how fertile futility is for it!
in this land where every living being or thing
is up for grabs or sale,
how headlong suffering is for it!

Earth, be mended
in the tears
of your seams, O ragged Earth,
be healed in your desire
for his body
through these tears. Mix him
with the thunders you've stored,
and with the rains,
the suns, the lightningcracks
and the strokes of your loving zodiac
wrap him home, wound in his friends'
never-ending memory of his ascendings.

Stockton Ave.

A Chinese woman raving
on the street
against black white yellow,
everyone trying to prostitute her
won't get away with it,
she want to beat up kill
everyone,
she want to marry police chief
he's no good but locks people up,
she gets down on one knee
on the sidewalk,
cries O buddha, christ — !
she begs them keep her
from killing herself.

A caucasian woman
outside a bar looks me
straight in the eye, calls
me
"a fucking pimp."
You are on my arm.
When I approach her,
ask her why,
she says,
"because you're a cab-driver."
Insane! I say

as the door opens
and a man comes out
who "knows, I'm
her husband."

"I Steal"

Scavenging's the way
I make a buck.
Pick my way thru
the garbage of the rich
for cardboard,
fabric-sampler folders,
odd papers, plastics.
Paint over them.
Send them to a man
who collects things
like that.
Get just enough to pay
for my hotel pad.

As for my meals,
they rhyme with "I feel"
at the end of the film
I WAS A FUGITIVE
FROM THE CHAIN GANG.
I know a million others,
brothers and sisters,
who say the same thing
as Paul Muni did
as they fade into the real:
"I steal."

Jesse

Keep me away from that bitch, he said, I mean
the priest came outta the church and she
pulled down her pants and pissed
right in front of him (the same padre
who slammed his doors on the foodline
on Good Friday two years ago)
and all night on the sidewalk in front
of the restaurant down there she was fuckin'
some guy, that bitch's in-
sane!

And he smiled half-terrified and put a brown five down on
my upcoming
palm.

Was Jesse. Is.
A raving equine beauty
with chestnut blonde hair
strong horse-teeth
in dirtywhite pants and cowboy boots
pushing a shoppingcart from Saroyan Alley up
                    to the church steps
two blocks away, and then back down, or these days
pulling a straw square basket with a leather leash attached
and a bag, her leather jacket, and yellow blanket
                    folded inside.

Sleeps with this one in the Alley,
that one in a doorway,
that one at the top of the steps
of St. Francis of Assisi,
panhandles the day for wine food cigarets,
and if you approach her her eyes go wild,
crazed-animal, caged-animal wild,
and if you touch her her clench her bite
hard down inside, the zing of fear
and violence,
love's a tooth,
her whole body a fang
impacted with thunder-rot,
who knows what else, and
driven! she, who pushes
or pulls, is
down on her butt between the men on a broken step
or in sidewalk sprawl, swigging laughing yelling:

"The pigs they're ignorant!"

Or up and haywire: "What a beautiful motorcycle
you have. Got any spare change?"

Or writing graffiti on the Alley wall.

Or hunched up in a doorway hugging a bottle
of wine to her chest, crowing, "When
oh when am I gonna get to the USA?"

Dancing Dave:
In Memoriam David Bronk, Poet

Dancing Dave, all of 35, is dead.
He won't come back from
a blue odee this time,
or gently put a finger to
his lips as his blond gangly form
floats along these streets and alleys,
or fire one-liner non-sequiturs
that always seem to fit into
the synchrony of these insane times,
or publish a poem of sensitive brilliance
in the journal between the ears.

Louie, the barker in front
of the girlie palace, says,
of all the dopers he's known
Dave was the gentlest,
never came on heavy from underneath,
always floated as if on LSD.
And Taura, who works in the Caffe Trieste,
bursts into tears in both
American and Portuguese,
knowing his eyes won't be
zooming in on the markings
on a ladybug's eggs anymore
down on a leaf in the park.

On a Line by Whitman

Suddenly there are no dead I want to remember
and my good love isn't desperate for a poem.
I'm beside myself with calm, stretched out
in my hotel room in San Francisco.
What must be done, the revolt in my pen,
has surrendered to this quiet
musing on nothing in particular.
The world's whizzing and whirling outside
but I'm more inclined to the hairs on my chest.
They've been there forty years or more
hardly noticed with so much to do,
and now they're turning grey.
Suddenly I feel I've missed them,
their red youth, the darkening way they attracted
many kisses to the flesh that lay beneath them.
I've really paid them little mind, let alone senses,
and now they'll soon be white, and what can I say?
That they didn't belong to me?
That they didn't mean very much?
When it comes to the body's poor old road,
every one must be a touch.

A Woman Gives Food

for Sarah Menefee

A woman gives food to a hungry hand.
The law says that it is contraband.
That law must fall, must lose its teeth,
must gum along the desolate streets
and come to the line where blessed soup
is smuggled in between the lips,
and know subversion for what it really is
and how this mean-lawed land is dead without it.

Oceanside: Oct. 30, 1986

Yesterday, after giving a reading
the day before in La Jolla,
I boarded an Amtrak
at Del Mar for Los Angeles.
Smoking car. Sparsely occupied.
At the next stop, Oceanside,
a woman boarded, passing
through the aisle.
White plastic bracelets
I thought she was selling
hung from her wrist.
Two seats behind me she addressed
a young man in Spanish:
Where are you from?
Los Angeles, I heard him say.
Her voice then rose to a cop-command:
"Venga con migo!" she said.
The young man rose, the handcuffs
were put on, and out of the coach
they went, he first, she following.
Five young students entered the coach,
babbling away. Two spoke Japanese,
one was Black, two wore earphones.
One of the girls said, "What I'm
listening to!" A young man
sitting directly behind me tried

to make a pass at her but she
couldn't hear him. The train
pulled out. On time.

Undone Day

You think I like being a dime bag in a doorway?
Living in a bottle in an alley?
Macho with the needlework of biceps?
You think I want this sweatshop of libernada?
Nowhere is the place where . . .
Immigrant from my own . . .
If I feel all the way to you, pais,
Que triste!

How small they want us
all, who never were
tall to begin with,

smaller than small — measly,
measlier than measly — crushed,
though our language can
hope so deeply and weep so full of stars.

Pobrecito Ricardo covered with bugs
where we found him,
a fleabag in a fleabag hotel,
how you say in spanish
even his death had to clear out
by seven in the morning.

Undone day
light in the eyes of the 18
as the boxcar door slammed shut
and night with fingernails
screaming against steel
the graffiti of
dying gasps on the inside of
the oven.

Undone day
of migrant wanderers pickpicking
pickpicking berries and crumbs
filling pittance baskets
under tortillas of smog.

Undone day
rubiado remembering how somewhere
tasted with all five senses,
how it was poor but like a leaflet
or a child in another's eyes.

Not this always Goliath of money towering
and myself a gob of saliva crazy for a sling,
not this broken fanta of youthful dignity,
not these disappeared *que pasos*.

Undone day
sesperado waiting for
my moan to reach the end of its decibel,
a hand to lift my earthquake
to the level of foundation,

a hope to organize my debris
into more than this little cell
going from one key to another
in search of the outside of in.

Diamanda

Diamanda Galas stands there
barechested under red lights
shrieking and wailing a dirge
for her brother dead of AIDS,
for all who've died of AIDS
and the many in the crowd
who are carrying the disease
under their jeans and leather.
She keens at the edge of the grave:
THERE ARE NO MORE TICKETS TO THE FUNERAL.
THE FUNERAL IS TOO CROWDED!
And nearing the end, her arm
flies up with a torch of a fist
and a cry: SODOMY OR DEATH!
And fists and cries respond,
and gasps at this woman who
whips words into highest decibels
galloping plateaus of pure lament
riding nails driven into the gospel
body of despair till it spurts
bleeding glossolalias of delirium.

This audience, this chorus
in a living mass grave,
these young given sex as deathrow cells,
these gay and straight and bisexual

rockers and punks,
artists and workers,
changelings of funk
Diamanda Galas is exorcising
from the raving precipice of her lips;
with a trilling diamond throat
she's lifting them out of the scourge,
attacking the youthiciders
in the orthodoxy of their rot,
tearing the eyes out of prayer
and the hair from bald lies
and the wheels from the axle of the Chariot
so it can't swing low;

because she's had it up to here and so have we
with the virus of evasion
and the plague of both houses
criminalizing bodies
and works of the young,
bleeping and robbing us of our apple,
leaving us pits in the pit;

she's had it up to here and so have we
with being made small of,
less than all of ourselves of,
being turned measly and cheap
driven to drink or drug or to thieve,
being born blue and shaking,
being cast out hungry to the street;

she's had it up to here and so have we,
up to here, up to here, and so
off with the heads of the heavy State!
Out of the grave she makes barricades!

O slaves of sense,
what more perfect
call to vengeance
than the lash of
the altitudes of
her breath!

We have nothing to lose but death.

Day of the Dead

My arm is heavy on your shoulder
because the feather is in you now.
I saw traffic through the bus window
stopped for blocks though there were no
gridlocks and the lights were green.
Why did you?
And me thinking: here it comes again,
when everything becomes paper-thin
and I say to myself, "I'm crazy
and walking through madness,"
and it's like you
could just stand and tear
existence in half, into quarters,
eighths, sixteenths, thirtytwos
except you're scared to begin
tearing, petrified that
if life really is only paper
you'll die of the void of air
once you start ripping it up;
so you don't, you just go on
till you can feel your body
coming back again, you don't know
how or why — a jostle of the bus,
a belch — suddenly I'm here,
you're sitting beside me,
it's over, we're still alive.

In Memoriam
The Jonestown Dead

It is that struck-dumb time
it is that agape
and face-down
it is that arms-around-each-other time
face-down

and for reading Celan
and Mayakovsky
Jozsef and Crane

it is that stammering for words time
in the midst of the thicket of lies
in the wave of the crime of democracy
hypocritized into shame
it is turkey handout time
and turkey no-blame

it is that struck-dumb time
bang the drumbone
beat the wings
eat the stuffings out of darkness
shake like cranberry

it is that struck-dumb time
it is that agape
it is that face-down time.
Fill your cup with wine.

Mayday

Do you remember when we went over and under
as we went around the Maypole tree
and braided it all in colorful ribbons
and sang songs and read poetry?

How young and innocent we were.
We never said Fuck on the trolley.
The only thing we burned was Hitler
Tojo and Mussolini grasshoppers.

Under the Maypole tree, O yes —
It was May Day and we braided it all up good.
How English we were in those days, really,
with all that My Country 'Tis of Thee.

When did it go away, I wonder,
and leave this skinny old stick
with faded ribbons round it, worth not
much more than 65 cents, I bet . . .

When

When I saw in the council chambers of the big city
the mouths of the council members
opening and coming down
on the fat sandwiches
that'd been delivered to their places,
coming down and chewing and leaning over talking
with half-stuffed mouths, or heads thrown back
laughing, their bellies chortling,
and all the while
one after another homeless person
stood not far from them
but far enough from them
before a microphone
requesting help for their most basic human wounds,
protesting against a syndrome without alternatives
except for skid-row hotels or a concentration
camp in the downtown desert; —

when I saw the indifference of this system
physically manifested
by those pigs of local government,
I thought: it can't be quick enough
that they're led to the sty they belong in;
it can't be quick enough
that they're forcibly removed
from the people's chambers

and replaced by human animals who, at least,
can smell the heartbreak
and the enduring dignity of the American people.
Those pigs are worse than the rottenest
blue pork at the bottom of garbage-can Los Angeles.
Hungry men and women never should have to be
subjected to their poisonously filthy mold.

The Future

The future as if nothing were
any different than the past (Pasolini
was right:

> La rivoluzione   The revolution
> non è più che   is no more than
> un sentimento   a feeling

whichever way one's sex leans,
a truth he died as much for
as for any set-up assassination
or assignation in the dark):

but that feeling of feminine, now,
isn't the chronic shmata of irascible dust and menses,
but a chthonic boom of living dignity,
and there will be
liberty's, not slavery's, children in the world for that;
for such feeling
is the spontaneous regeneration of the soul-cell
sold out to the microminimost
chromosome in the nucleus of Nothing,
which nonetheless, when it so much as twitches,
will be a spit in the eye of the old dead God,
and, in that sense, yes, a salivary gesture,
the deliverance of a righteous little gob
of oystery spittle into the dead sea
of pharaonic lies — the three (the men, the feeling

of feminine, and the child that is the godless
act itself) can and will spread
a table for the future feast of existence
without any crucifixions in the wings.

Tornado Woman

It spins, it whirls, yet roots deep down
in "the spiral of the gene":
Meridel's tornado writing.
The circle of hands, the web stretching
from Sirius to the shining carborundum
in the black earth of the Dakotas:
the dinosaur thunder of Meridel.
O haywire concentration on the tendons
of the people, straining toward
the redress of wounds:
the propagandance of Meridel Le Sueur.

Sahaykhwisay

That he in quotes was named Sahaykhwisay
and the excitement touching upon
such a matter even now 2/3
of a century later
since women other
than my own woman are, in part,
in their parts, as I am gone
to poor river, lesbian
transvestites being, like her,
farmers and hunters
and sometimes hookers,
"rich enough to wear shoes"
the other Mohaves said of her,
who insisted she was a man
despite her breasts, which
were ample, who was a shaman
of venereal disease, and so,
they said, "lucky in love."

I know a woman like her
and I have seen two women
sucking each other inside
the hooch of my cock.
Sahaykhwisay chased girls,
the free young shrubberies first.
She made them wives;

they'd love and drink and
the Mohaves in the Needles
Cafe would ridicule. They'd leave her,
and Sahaykhwisay would down
strong liquor with the men
even as the hair of her women
was torn all over the floor.

It was going after married women
she met rape
from Ha'kwa
and afterward she courted no more.
She lived with a man, Tch'um.
She fucked the ghosts of her old loves
in dreams and where desires
come together.
When Tch'um died, she fucked
his son and another Indian
and they all went 30 miles north
to work together drunk.

Sahaykhwisay wanted her girls,
Sahaykhwisay drank to her ghosts.
She would not get out,
she could not get in.
Sahaykhwisay ran her tongue
along the flank of a filly
in the moonlight.
She wailed she was a shaman
and lucky in love.
She cried for the cunts of Needles

and wore thick black paint.
The son of Tch'um
one drunken night
threw her into the Colorado.
She did not want to swim.
Buzzards told some people where
two weeks later.
She was cremated in Needles as a witch.

This was as it was,
at the turn of the century.
Leather Feces made a drawing
of a bird with her ashes and the fire's.
The sky was blue, the clouds tipped pink.
Then the machine began
to hand out faces.

Haiti Now

They are standing around on dusty corners
human drums that should be fed,
but there is no food.

A swollen misery is a child
and the basket on a woman's head
is carrying a few eels of potato.

There is talking, there is gossip
there is committee work, *coumbites*
of placards and graffiti criers,
and the talk talks itself into sauces,
and the gossip stirs itself into spices,
and the organizing heats up
like a loaf of bread,
but there is no bread,
no food
and the people cannot read the leaflets.

But there is talk, the *tiyediol*,
the seeds of the second uprising.
The people know it is only a matter of time,
that the cops and army will not
be able to hold back
the surge of misery demanding an end to misery.

For now, though the dynasty is over,
the zombies of the deathshead rule,
have put on the khaki of legitimate thugs.
But the people know their voodoo
all the way back to Boukman,
they are standing around on dusty corners
human drums that are going to be fed
the instruments of their liberation,
women who have come forward
with political Ezilis in their eyes,
and look, there,
at that wall of graffiti,
a little boy showing his tiny brother
how to read, letter by letter,
Aba mize!
Aba gouveman makoutes!
Aba merikan imperialism!
Viva sosyalism Ayisyen!

In Memoriam Dolores Ibarurri

died Nov. 12, 1989

As she was passing,
La Passionaria,
as she was passing through
the 95 petals
of the red rose
of her death
in Madrid,

the cry she'd composed
— No Pasaran! —
sang out of every bullet
fired by the FMLN
guerrillas in the streets
and from the barricades
of San Salvador.

You're Being Assed

To consent to the plunder.
To empty your pockets of rage,
along with your other belongings,
before you enter your infinite cell.
To sell with the best of them,
to kiss principle on the cheek,
pat principle on the ass,
send principle to the corner
of Sasparilla & Hooya Streets.
To open a stripjoint in Nevsky Prospekt.
To see that there's plenty
of moonrock in Leningrad.
To junk out the Baltics,
waste Poland with ice,
bring back pebbles from Moscow
and sell them for enormous prices.
Hammersickle teeshirts all over the USA
sponsored by McDonald's near the Bolshoi.
Nedra Flunk will introduce
the Raisa Dildo.
We'll all live to a hundred
with fleece as white as snow.

Organize the Heart

When a woman is eating out of a garbage can,
not a woman in a poem eating out of a garbage can,
not a woman in a painting or film eating out of a garbage can,
when a woman is eating out of a garbage can,
that's censorship.

A woman eating out of a garbage can
or curled up in a doorway,
a man sprawled out on a sidewalk,
a child in a cardboard hovel
are censorship victims of a system of competitive profiteering
more obscene than the most obscene image imaginable,
more rabid in its barking for lucre
than the most tawdry porn recordable.

When a woman has to eat out of a garbage can
and a man rummage the night for a rag of space
and a child shiver with bowl or cup for coins,
all poems, all paintings and films,
whatever their content,
drop to the street,
organize the heart
to resist the smug and vicious indifference
of systemic decay parading as virtue,
become house, beds, warm food, good cheer,

first in the heart's solitude,
then in the mind's collective demand,
then with bodies' unanimous storm
transform censorship into the liberty
that never stops housing and feeding all.

The Body Holocaust

On the surface, then,
and for a while anyway,
skid the word, skip it along, pebble-by
syllable-wise, tuning up, so to speak,
the fire that cannot yet be
because the smoke from the old
crematorium of yourself
hasn't altogether come seeping
out of the corners of your mouth;
because the smell of ash hasn't utterly
vanished from the crook of your neck
or the vise of your thighs
or the mingle-mashle of your breath;
and the skin of your death
hasn't completely released
its chokehold from your soul.
You still believe in depth without a charge,
in hope without a hole in it the size of a barrel.
You still believe you'll always find a leaf
against humiliation, that there really *are*
faucets that don't run with nazi water;
that innocence transcends the gangbang of plugs
and wires jammed into all the orifices
of the human form; that the sun is inevitable
because your toke just told you so
and it doesn't get any nakeder than that;

and that there will be such recovery
when we can all have found . . .
when finally we can all be founded,
and the question doesn't immediately rise:
when *can* we all be founded?
and the answer not immediately resound:
Never! Never, after those smokestacks,
can the soul not be hounded!

Shining Mourning

Those "inconspicuous tears"
of loss perhaps dearest —

                how long you fought
                to with-hold them
                from me, angel.

Now they simply appear
in the desert of my face.

I go about as ever
but they are there
in the desert of my face.

They mark me: shining
mourning.

All day and night it is:
shining mourning.

Nor is there a why,
nor a because.
Comes the image of you —
no, the image of you
does not come,
there is no image of you
but heartbeat.
My heart beats
and the waters rise.
They rise and cast

    your radiance
at the sills of my eyes
where you look out from.
    Twice, and shining.
The camel comes from afar
    and drinks from them.
It is the camel's way
of kissing you.
The nomad falls to his knees
and drinks from them.
It is the nomad's way
of kissing you.
You go with the camel,
you ride its back,
yet remain at the sills
of my eyes, radiance.
You go with the nomad,
happily hand in hand
with the nomad,
yet remain at the sills
of my eyes, radiance.

I thought death
had dried up in me
after the flood
of memory had subsided.
But this one is so alive,
I can moisten
anything parched,

anyone cracked,
anywhere thirsty
very naturally,
very inconspicuously.

All day and all night:
shining mourning.

The Breeze of Peace

*In memory of Richard Breeze, who immolated
himself in San Francisco at the outset of
the war with Iraq*

O suicided Breeze,
your body ablaze on the corner
of Francisco and Franklin Streets

O immolated Breeze
still moaning through the streets
of burning hair and blistered everythings

O brother Breeze,
may memory of you stir embers of hope
and spin the particles in the depths
of war's molecules into dervishes
round the sun of peace, and may we
feed from its light at last like fishes
nibbling in a great galactic sea.

The Heat

Touch me where it hurts
allover
with war again.

The cops have arrested
our pots, pans, and stoves,
and broken our feeding tent
in the Civic Center.

And told Jack, who simply
was tightening his belt
on Polk St, to
"do it in a bathroom."

And told Fanny they'll bust her
she sells her little things,
and painted drawings,
on Vallejo St anymore (we all
loved standing on that slope
with her, shooting the breeze).

The roust the club the dog the hose.

I don't care if they are workers,
I'll never Sir-suck up to them.

Khafji Pushes Police
Finger Towards Triggers.

House and cafe windows on the Beach
fill with old informers.

It's the war again, our hands
clenched in pockets, walking;
our eyes, shoe-shame-down
or who's behind . . .

Taut-spine, a
violent
siren.

Requiem for the War Dead

We will not know, we've been told, who they are,
the sons and daughters of the working class.
Strewn across the sands, they'll be
gathered, labelled, bagged and flown
to a twilight hangar in Delaware.

Gracie Beavers
Shawn Bermingham
Christopher Berry
Jimmy Burks
William Butters
Donna Conklin
Warren Dillard
Peter De Dolce
Stephen De Dolce
Charles Fountain
Danny Hitchcock
Stephen Richard Legro
Rutherford Loneman
Anthony Lopez
Bruce Martin
John Wesley More
Roxanna Peters
Susan Jan Reddy
Chena Risley
William Socia

Howard Stansell
Ray Thompson

They could be the above, who died
in attacks on the heart,
winter-whipped to death,
debris found at the bottom of flights
of stairs in TL hotels,
hit and run-overs,
slumped frozen panhandlers,
lesionaires of AIDS
drilled by hypothermia under cardboard
or in abandoned cars,
riddled with pneumonia,
barraged by waves till drowned
in a beach dug-out,
battered for a swig or some change,
lung-arrested
brain-arrested,
heart-arrested
and iced.

Might as well be the above;
for all we know,
they are the above,
and below —
                    a potter's field
of an arlington
growing and growing
the no-one's rose
of the wars' homeless.

Uniform Terror

The way they bombed hell
out of them when they were down,
the criminal Iraqis,

and went on bombing
till fear became worldwide
collateral damage.

"Saddam is a sandnigger"
— graffiti in a Bakersfield
Arco toilet.

Down the road, the way
they beat hell out of a Black
named King on the ground.

The uniform
terror settling into even
this haiku's syllables.

Pitiless Pieta

The texture
of the rubble
and child.

Slabs of shame,
stone-in and stone-out, the massive
tonnage on our hearts

which shall grow thick
hair allover our bodies
shall walk on all fours
our necks grown long,
our bodies humped, there
will be nothing but endless
embers of sand, water
has stopped existing,
only death is a bowl
filled with a nectar we
are competing to gulp
down . . .

The Night

for Cornelius Cardew,
People's Composer

There is a night that does not fall
when the sun dies,
that does not belong to the clock
yet is worn
like an invisible armband of a
millennial moment.
A child is born and wears it,
no matter he suckles in joy
or wails at a starving dug.
There is a night-music burned
into the soul of every atom,
a music that belongs to the motion
of that endless night
so excruciating in its truth,
so elemental in its resonance
of dissonant despair,
it is rarely performed,
it is unbearable with grief;
its skizzenbooks lie in boxes
in cellars or attics of houses
where people listen to sounds
of popular liberation, musics
that carry them from one
copacetic joy to the next
through their days.

Sometimes this other music
will manage to find its way out
of a darkness that amounts to subversion:
a record will be made, a concert performed,
it will rise and present itself
as the night that underlies
all the nights so desperate for breath
sounds are made to fill up every hole
so that this other music, this other
night, not be sounded.
Sometimes it is; sometimes it finds
through a crack in the headlong
rush of survival
a solitude that calls it forth,
a conjunction of sorrows that needs it
and would knead it by means of
the fluttering hands of their hearts
into a bread that really is present.
Then we can hear it emerging
with fingers scraping
on the ceilings of our own screaming, gagging mouths,
with rifle-butts on brains and raisin-eyes floating
in sockets of blood,
with riddles of bullets down the back of a child,
with the sounds of ankles being broken,
with the crackles of immolation
and the winebottle of gasoline drunk
by a collapsing wall.
It emerges, it brings the perennial of darkness
close to our nostrils.
We smell that night of death, which triumphed and died,

and the time it will take
to die of it:
the rest of our lives.

When We Tear Tomorrow Open

When there aren't enough pencils to go 'round,
a teacher's forced to pay for them out of her pocket,
she has children, they need
to write.

A mother's relieved in quotes of her hungry kids
and put into the slammer for defrauding in quotes
welfare of 130 bux.

No wonder, so easily, the teenager's "I'm outta here!"
and meaning a lethal hotshot in the arm or a swing
over the rail of the (Golden) Gate: sheer plod does not
make sillion shine, just a leftover tinfoiled sandwich
in a garbage bin.

"Kafka wrote this building," Keith McHenry said
standing in the marble corridor of 850 Bryant awaiting
the trial of Sarah Menefee for having given free food
"without a permit."

And Jackson smashed by the cops into a window
and King savaged by bats held by men in blue sheets
in the gutter.

The glass the cuts
the bruises the cuts
the indignities and still
the collateral cuts
and more coming
and more . . .

What the hell are we in this for?
Our good name?
The system's already numbered it.
Our dying shmatas?
Our clear thoughts about the end of western civilization?
Your hopeless feud with the devil?
My foot?

I want some breakneck speed to wrap me 'round
in a typhoon of people's rights.
No more half-assed splinter-routes to a trickledown reform.
No more gunpowder idea without feet in the real.

I'm talking about yesterday's calamity and how the law
comes down with its teeth closing out the story.
Gets in the way of the future.
Upholds its relation to property.
Leaves its scars on every soul.
A ticket, a warrant, an injunction, the sweep òf its
foolish liberty. To be a cellular phone
to a corporation.

Alright, getting this off raw, without much to swing on.
The lights *are* going out in the west.
The whole pack's slivered into insidiously
                    shepherded individuals
chopped into instances, cyclical What's up? Hi there!
and other one-liney spots.

Hopeless stuff, crackbrained
liberty. Nothing fits right
foot and the left is
dead.

We'd better organize and fight together and put some real
class in that anarchy it's fitted us all out with,
because you can virtually smell the clanking
military might right in your neighborhood.

When we struggle together,
from the very first ascent,
the lash will be stayed, the club paralyzed in the air.

And when we go deeper together,
deeper than sex or race, deeper than the ancestral
faces of the dead with their souls of blood
and the tenderness that curls clear down
in the spiral of the genes,

when we tear tomorrow open
and all together now throw our lives into our voice
and our voices into the song,

it cannot hold us back,
it must give way (it's already crumbling
                              of its own exploitations),

we can't but be
what all this human injustice
was meant to be toppled by,

and it will be,
we know it will,
we who have mastered
the smithereens.

Song

Lift it!
Lift its body
spat-upon and scorned
these many months.
Haven't you ever
lifted
a woman fallen to the street,
a man lying on the sidewalk,
a child ganged-up on,
arms on the ground
protecting his head
from the kicks?

The song's the same.
Lift it! Raise it up.
Let its cuts and wounds
have some air.
It's not dead.
It'll never die.
Beaten, chained, slandered,
— look, it's reaching
for your voice.
Lift it.
Let it rise in its place.
The Internationale
shall be the human race.